GW00733325

CHIP *for* everyone

200155716

This guidance is issued by the Health and Safety Executive. Following the guidance is not compulsory and you are free to take other action. But if you do follow the guidance you will normally be doing enough to comply with the law. Health and Safety inspectors seek to secure compliance with the law and may refer to this guidance as illustrating good practice.

C ontents

UNDERSTANDING CHIP

1   This guide is intended to help business understand the basic requirements of the Chemicals (Hazard Information and Packaging for Supply) Regulations 2002[1] (known as CHIP 3 or, more simply, as CHIP). It tells you what you have to do and what you do not have to do. It replaces the earlier *CHIP 2 for everyone.*[2]

2   A free short introduction to CHIP is published separately.[7] Details of it and other HSE publications on CHIP are in the references at the back of this book. The Health and Safety Executive's (HSE) CHIP website (www.hse.gov.uk/hthdir/noframes/chip/chip1.htm) has news and background material on CHIP.

What have you heard?

3   If you are reading this you probably supply chemicals. The type may vary from commodity chemicals in bulk to household cleaning products in small packages. You may be a major manufacturer or a retailer selling products. If you are a small employer, your company may not have laboratories or chemical testing facilities. It may have some technical expertise, but not much. You may have heard of CHIP. You may also have heard that it is long, complicated and technical. You are feeling rather confused, if not anxious.

4   If this sounds familiar, then this guide is for you. It aims to give you a basic introduction to CHIP. It will explain how the Regulations work and how they will be updated. It will help you decide what you should do about CHIP and whether you should get help. You may decide that *CHIP for everyone* is all you need.

What is CHIP?

5   CHIP is law which applies to suppliers of dangerous chemicals. Its purpose is to protect people and the environment from the effects of these chemicals by requiring suppliers to give information and to package them safely. The idea is that if people know about the dangers of a chemical, and what they can do to avoid them, they will be less likely to harm themselves, others or the environment.

What does CHIP do?

6   CHIP requires the supplier of a dangerous chemical to:

- **identify the hazards (dangers)** of the chemical (this is known as 'classification');
- **package the chemical safely**; and
- **give information about the hazards** to their customers (usually by means of information on the package (eg a label) and, if supplied for use at work, a safety data sheet).

These are known as supply requirements. 'Supply' is defined as making a chemical available to another person. Manufacturers, importers, distributors, wholesalers and retailers are examples of suppliers.

An overview of CHIP

7   We'll begin by making a general survey of CHIP and then look at particular aspects in greater detail in other parts of this guide. For now we shall:

- specify the documents which make up the CHIP package;
- see which chemicals CHIP applies to;
- describe briefly how CHIP works;
- consider the simplest case of supply; and
- say something about where CHIP comes from and why it keeps changing.

Along the way, we'll give definitions of commonly-used terms and list CHIP's categories of danger. Finally, we'll mention some other areas of chemical legislation which are related to CHIP.

The CHIP package

8   This consists of the Regulations themselves and a number of associated documents, which contain supporting detail or explanatory material. As a supplier you may need some or all of these documents. See references section.

Regulations

9   The Regulations are the Chemicals (Hazard Information and Packaging for Supply) Regulations 2002 and any later amending Regulations.* The Regulations set out the framework of the CHIP scheme and can be bought from the Stationery Office or viewed on its website (www.legislation.hmso.gov.uk/stat.htm).

Approved documents

10   Much of CHIP's technical detail is in two documents defined in the Regulations:

- the Approved Supply List (ASL);[3] and
- the Approved Classification and Labelling Guide (ACLG).[4]

The ASL gives obligatory classifications and labels for several thousand commonly-supplied substances. The ACLG gives rules for classifying and labelling chemicals not listed in the ASL. Anyone creating or checking classifications and labels should have access to these documents. They are published by HSE Books and revised from time to time. (See the List of Commonly Used Terms on page 7 for the meaning of 'substance' and 'chemical'.)

---

*   Details of the most up-to-date documents are on the CHIP website at
    www.hse.gov.uk/hthdir/noframes/chip/chip2.htm (see also paragraph 2 above)

Approved Codes of Practice

11 Still more information is to be found in an Approved Code of Practice (ACOP) and a European Directive:

- *The compilation of safety data sheets*;[5] and
- Annex V to the Dangerous Substances Directive.[6]

The first is published by HSE Books and gives guidance on CHIP's safety data sheet (SDS) requirements. It should be referred to by anyone drawing up or checking SDS. The second describes laboratory test methods for determining the properties of dangerous chemicals.

Explanatory documents

12 In addition to this guide there are three other advisory publications on CHIP which can be obtained from HSE Books or viewed on HSE's website. They are the booklet: *Idiot's guide to CHIP*,[7] and two leaflets: *Read the label*,[8] and *Why do I need a safety data sheet?*[9]

Which chemicals does CHIP apply to?

13 CHIP applies to most chemicals. The exceptions, which are identified in regulation 3(1), are specialised chemicals such as cosmetics, medicines, wastes and several others - all of which are covered by other regulations. If, after reading regulation 3, you are not sure whether CHIP applies to your chemical, contact HSE's Infoline (Tel: 08701 545500).

How CHIP works

14 CHIP is basically a set of dos and don'ts which apply to people who supply chemicals. Its fundamental requirement is for you (the supplier) to decide, using a set of rules, whether a chemical is dangerous or not. If you decide the chemical is dangerous (ie 'classified') then a number of further requirements will be triggered. If you decide the chemical is not dangerous then nothing further is required, unless the chemical falls into one of the special cases in the Regulations. These are explained in regulations 5 and 10 and in Part II of Schedule 5 of the Regulations.

15 While reading what follows it may be helpful to refer to the table of commonly used terms on page 7, the table of categories of danger on page 8 and the flow chart on page 9.

Classification

16 If you have decided that a chemical is dangerous then you will need to:

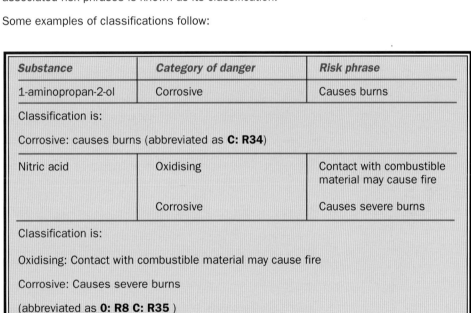

- place the chemical into a category of danger (possibly more than one); and
- qualify the category of danger by assigning a risk phrase (R-phrase).

The standardised description of a dangerous chemical's hazards (dangers) by means of categories of danger and associated risk phrases is known as its classification. Some examples of classifications follow:

Substance	Category of danger	Risk phrase
1-aminopropan-2-ol	Corrosive	Causes burns
Classification is:		
Corrosive: causes burns (abbreviated as **C: R34**)		
Nitric acid	Oxidising	Contact with combustible material may cause fire
	Corrosive	Causes severe burns
Classification is:		
Oxidising: Contact with combustible material may cause fire		
Corrosive: Causes severe burns		
(abbreviated as **O: R8 C: R35**)		

The classification is the basis for the chemical's label, safety data sheet and packaging. If it is wrong then all of these will probably be wrong as well. CHIP makes it an offence to supply a dangerous chemical before it has been properly classified.

The Approved Supply List

17 Many commonly-supplied dangerous substances have already been classified and are listed with their labelling and other information in the ASL. If you supply these substances you must use this information.

18 If the chemical is a substance which is not listed in the ASL, or if it is a preparation, then you must classify it yourself. We'll look at this in more detail later in the guide but for now we can say that it involves:

- **in the case of a substance**, gathering available data on its dangerous properties (there is no requirement to carry out tests) and then classifying it by comparing that data with criteria in the ACLG; or
- **in the case of a preparation**, using either one or both of the following:
  - working out the classification of the preparation from the classifications of its constituent substances (this procedure is known as the **conventional method**); or
  - testing the preparation to obtain data on it and then proceeding as above using the ACLG.

The simplest case of supply

19 Say you buy a chemical and supply it to others but you do not do anything with the chemical - you do not mix, react, process or reformulate it. The chemical should have been properly classified before it reached you and if this is the case you can use that classification when you come to supply it on. This is an easy and usually reliable way of classifying a chemical, particularly if the chemical is a common one and you know the supplier is competent. However, you should be aware that CHIP makes you, the supplier, responsible for the classification you use even if it is the work of someone else. In such cases you need to carry out some checks to confirm the classification.

20 If you want to use a classification given by your supplier, you should make appropriate enquiries about the classification. If you know your suppliers and have confidence in their ability, only simple checks may be needed. Some of the checks you could carry out are:

- if it is a substance, see whether it is in the ASL (many commonly supplied substances are);
- use your common sense and experience about the classification (an extreme (but not unknown) example would be if an acid commonly known to cause burns had not been classified as 'corrosive' - this would obviously be wrong);
- compare it to the classification of similar chemicals;
- find out from your supplier what information they used to classify it or ask other people competent in this area that you trust; and
- check the classification with other published information.

You should make similar checks if you use another supplier's safety data sheet or label information.

COMMONLY USED TERMS

Hazard	The inherent dangerous properties of a chemical.
Risk	The likelihood of the hazardous properties of a chemical causing harm (to people or the environment). Unlike the hazard, which is a fixed property of the chemical, the risk depends on the circumstances of use, etc and is controllable.
Category of danger	A description of hazard type.
Classification	Precise identification of the hazard of a chemical by assigning a category of danger and a risk phrase using set criteria.
Risk phrase (R-phrase)	A standard phrase which gives simple information about the hazards of a chemical in normal use.
Safety phrase (S-phrase)	A standard phrase which gives advice on safety precautions which may be appropriate when using a chemical.
Substance	A chemical element or one of its compounds, including any impurities.
Preparation	A mixture of substances.
Chemical	A generic term for substances and preparations.
Tactile warning devices (TWDs)	A small raised triangle applied to a package intended to alert the blind and visually impaired to the fact that they are handling a container of a dangerous chemical.
Child resistant fastenings (CRFs)	A closure which meets certain standards intended to protect young children from accessing the hazardous contents of a package.
Chain of supply	The successive ownership of a chemical as it passes from manufacturer to its ultimate user.
Approved Code of Practice (ACOP)	Advice prepared by HSC on how to comply with the requirements of the law. An ACOP has special legal status. If you are prosecuted for breach of health and safety legislation, and it is proven you have not followed the relevant provisions of the ACOP, a court will find you at fault, unless you can show that you have complied with the law in some other way.

Categories of danger

	Category of danger	Symbol letter	Indication of danger	Symbol (orange background)
Physico-chemical	Explosive	**E**	Explosive	
	Oxidising	**O**	Oxidising	
	Extremely flammable	**F+**	Extremely flammable	
	Highly flammable	**F**	Highly flammable	
	Flammable	**none**	**none**	**none**
Health	Very toxic	**T+**	Very toxic	
	Toxic	**T**	Toxic	
	Harmful	**Xn**	Harmful	
	Corrosive	**C**	Corrosive	
	Irritant	**Xi**	Irritant	
	Sensitising (by inhalation)	**Xn**	Harmful	
	Sensitising (by skin contact)	**Xi**	Irritant	
	Carcinogenic *Categories 1 and 2*	**T**	Toxic	
	Carcinogenic *Category 3*	**Xn**	Harmful	
	Mutagenic *Categories 1 and 2*	**T**	Toxic	
	Mutagenic *Category 3*	**Xn**	Harmful	
	Toxic to reproduction *Categories 1 and 2*	**T**	Toxic	
	Toxic to reproduction *Category 3*	**Xn**	Harmful	
Environmental	Dangerous for the environment	**N**	Dangerous for the environment	
	Dangerous for the environment*	**none**	**none**	**none**

* Where only environmental R-phrases assigned are R52 or R53 or R52, 53

How CHIP works

Is the chemical a substance or preparation?

Is it dangerous?

NO

YES

CHIP does not apply*

CHIP requires it to be classified

Assign categories of danger and a risk phrase

Provide:
- safety data sheet
- label
- safe packaging
- child-resistant closures and tactile danger warnings if needed

---

* But see regulations 9 and 11 of CHIP for preparations which are special cases.

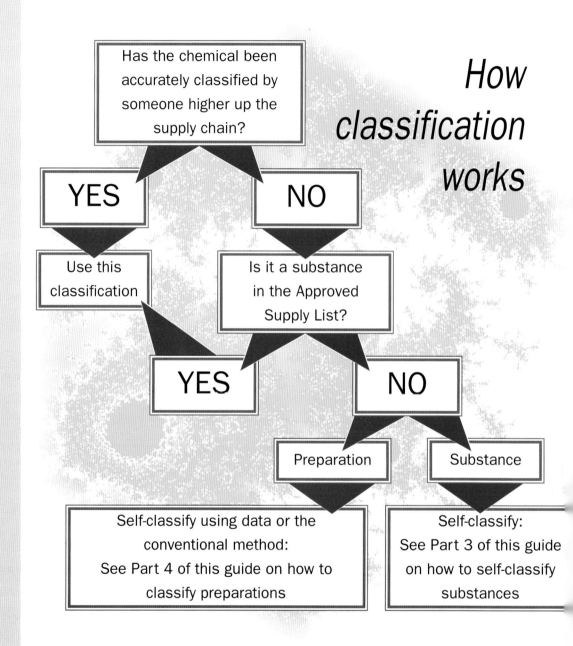

How classification works

Has the chemical been accurately classified by someone higher up the supply chain?

YES

NO

Use this classification

Is it a substance in the Approved Supply List?

YES

NO

Preparation

Substance

Self-classify using data or the conventional method:
See Part 4 of this guide on how to classify preparations

Self-classify:
See Part 3 of this guide on how to self-classify substances

Where CHIP
omes from and
why it keeps
changing

21   CHIP is based on European Directives, which apply to all EU and European Economic Area (EEA) Countries. The Directives are intended to create a level playing field in the supply of dangerous chemicals by ensuring that suppliers in each country are subject to the same requirements. The Directives are under constant review and changes are made from time to time. Whenever changes occur to the Directives (typically about once each year), CHIP has to be changed as well.

Updating CHIP

22   Usually we update CHIP by issuing a short set of amending Regulations which modify but do not replace the main set (known as the principal Regulations). When major changes occur, however, the principal Regulations are revised. At the time this guide was written, the story was as follows.

- The first set of principal Regulations (CHIP or CHIP 1) was introduced in 1993.[10]
- CHIP 1 was replaced in 1994 by new principal Regulations (CHIP 2),[11] which were amended in 1996, 1997, 1998, 1999 and 2000.
- CHIP 2 and all of its amending Regulations were replaced in 2002 by the Chemicals (Hazard Information and Packaging for Supply) Regulations 2002 (CHIP 3).

In this guide we use the word 'CHIP' to mean whatever set of CHIP Regulations is currently in force.

23   Changes to CHIP are often limited to the technical information in the ASL and the ACLG. As a result, amending Regulations usually do little more than formally introduce and give legal effect to new editions of these publications.

24   We now finish this part of the guide by looking briefly at some other areas of chemical legislation to which CHIP is related.

CHIP doesn't only
affect people who
supply chemicals

25   CHIP is not about the use, storage, disposal, etc of chemicals. However, the laws governing these matters often need to take into account how dangerous a chemical is and to do this they may use their CHIP classifications. As a result they may be affected by changes to CHIP. For example, a change in the CHIP classification of a substance may alter the measures needed under the Control of Substances Hazardous to Health Regulations 1999 (COSHH),[12] to control the risks arising from the use of that substance in the workplace.*

---

*HSE has published guidance to help firms using chemicals to control the health risks to their employees better and comply with the law. *COSHH essentials: easy steps to control chemicals* takes employers through a risk assessment to find the control measures they need and gives practical examples in a series of control guidance sheets (see details at end of this guide). The starting point for the assessment is your safety data sheet. You can use this guidance to help the firms you supply to find the control measures they need to protect health. You may also find it helpful yourself.

CHIP and carriage regulations

26 Carriage of dangerous chemicals ('carriage' means the way a chemical is transported, for example, by road or by rail) is not the same thing as supply. There are extensive regulations dealing with carriage, which have their own scheme of classification, packaging and labelling/marking. In some cases a transport label may be used instead of the label required by CHIP, and vice versa. If you want to know about the law on carriage you should look at the HSE publications:

- *Are you involved in the carriage of dangerous goods by road or rail?*[13]
- *Carriage of dangerous goods explained: Part 1 Guidance for consignors of dangerous goods by road and rail (classification, packaging and labelling and provision of information).*[14]

CHIP and EC Regulation 2455/92

27 CHIP is British law and applies only to people in Great Britain.* CHIP does not apply to exports to other countries in the European Union (EU) although the Directives on which it is based do. Although other Member States' (MS) law is based on the same EU legislation it is sometimes interpreted in slightly different ways, so if you are supplying a chemical to another MS then you need to check that MS's law. CHIP also does not apply to exports to countries outside the EU. This is subject to EC Regulation 2455/92[15] which requires, amongst other things, that such exports should be:

- packaged and labelled in the same way as if they were being marketed within the EU; and
- labelled in the language of the country of destination if practicable. (There is no requirement for a safety data sheet although it is good practice to include one.)

28 In addition, EC Regulation 2455/92[15] includes two lists of dangerous chemicals which if imported to, or exported from the EU, are subject to special requirements. More information on this can be found on HSE's website at www.hse.gov.uk/hthdir/noframes/pic/pic1.htm.

Summary of key points

- CHIP applies to suppliers of most chemicals.
- It obliges the supplier of a chemical to:
    - identify the hazards;
    - provide information on the hazards (labels and safety data sheets); and
    - provide safe packaging.
- A supplier may use others' classifications, etc, provided common-sense care is taken to check their validity.

---

*Northern Ireland has its own CHIP Regulations. These mirror the British Regulations and refer to the same approved documents. For more information contact the Health and Safety Executive for Northern Ireland.

CLASSIFYING AND LABELLING SUBSTANCES WHICH ARE IN THE APPROVED SUPPLY LIST

29 Say you make or import substances (see paragraphs 40 to 43 in Part three for the meaning of 'substance'), or have doubts about the classification and labelling of substances you have received from your supplier. If the substances are reasonably common they may be in the ASL with information on their classifications, labels, etc. In fact, if you are supplying these substances, you have to use this information.

How to find a substance in the ASL

30 First, make sure that you have the current version - check the CHIP pages of HSE's website or contact the HSE InfoLine. If you don't have it already, you can get a copy of the ASL from HSE Books.

31 Part I of the ASL lists substances in alphabetical order by name (where the ASL recognises more than one name for a substance it will be listed under each name). Note, however, that complex coal and oil-derived substances are collected together in groups under 'c' (for coal tar products) or 'p' (for petroleum substances). Having found the substance, read off the classification and labelling information, referring to Part V of the ASL for full texts of the R- and S-phrases. For example:

Classifying sodium carbonate using the ASL

32 Sodium carbonate is found in Part I under 's'. Its classification is given as:

Xi: R36

Here 'Xi' stands for 'Irritant' (the category of danger) and 'R36' for 'Irritating to eyes' (the R-phrase). Together these define the hazardous nature of the substance.

33　Glutaraldehyde (also known as glutaral) is found under 'g' and as 1,5-pentanedial under 'p' (you may use any of these names, but not others, on the package label). The classification is given as:

T: R23/25 C: R34 R42/43 N: R50

Glutaraldehyde has many more dangerous properties than sodium carbonate and so its classification is more complex. It has been placed into four categories of danger. These (with their abbreviations) are:

● 　 Toxic (T);

● 　 Corrosive (C);

● 　 Sensitising (R42/43); and

● 　 Dangerous for the environment (N).

The respective R-phrases (with their abbreviations) are:

● 　 Toxic by inhalation and if swallowed (R23/25);

● 　 Causes burns (R34);

● 　 May cause sensitisation by inhalation and skin contact (R42/43); and

● 　 Very toxic to aquatic organisms (R50).

34   The label for a chemical is based on its classification. The ASL gives the following labelling information for glutaraldehyde:

T, N

R23/25, 34, 42/43, 50

S(1/2), 26, 36/37/39, 45, 61

203-856-5

T and N are 'symbol letters'. They do not go on the label but specify the hazard warning **symbols** and associated **indications of danger** that do. The full set of symbol letters and corresponding symbols and indications of danger is set out in the table of categories of danger on page 8. (Note that only the symbol-letter corresponding to the most severe health effect (in this case, T) appears in the labelling information.)

R23/25, 34, etc specify the **R-phrases**. These are the same phrases that appear in the classification. The role of an R-phrase in the classification is to define a hazard, but on the label its purpose is to warn people of it.

S(1/2), 26, etc specify the **S-phrases**. These give advice on how to avoid or deal with dangers. For example, S61 is 'Avoid release to the environment. Refer to special instructions/safety data sheet'.

The full text of each R- and S-phrase (which can be found in Part V of the ASL) is required on the label, the abbreviations should not be used.

203-856-5 is the **EC number** for glutaraldehyde. An EC number is always needed on labels for substances. In addition, the words 'EC label' must appear on the label, if the substance is listed in the ASL.

35   There is no prescribed format for a CHIP label so the following illustration is only a possible layout. You can see the two warning symbols, the two indications of danger, the four R-phrases and the five S-phrases.

Glutaraldehyde		
 **Toxic**	 **Dangerous for the environment**	Toxic by inhalation and if swallowed Causes burns May cause sensitisation by inhalation and by skin contact Very toxic to aquatic organisms Keep locked up and out of the reach of children In case of contact with eyes, rinse immediately with plenty of water and seek medical advice Wear suitable protective clothing, gloves and eye/face protection
EC label 203-856-5		In case of accident or if you feel unwell seek medical advice immediately (show the label where possible) Avoid release to the environment. Refer to special instructions/safety data sheet
Supplied by: Dyson-Warner Chemicals Ltd, Dyne Close, Blainey, Ryanshire CH1P 3EX 0207 7170000		

Additional information

36   The ASL entry for glutaraldehyde, under the heading 'Conc', gives specific concentration limits for that substance. This information is relevant to the classification of preparations containing glutaraldehyde as a constituent. Its use is explained in Part four of this guide.

Many substance entries have annotations such as 'Note E' or 'Note 4'. These notes are very important and should always be considered. Their individual meanings are explained in the introduction and Part V of the ASL.

Summary of key points

- The ASL gives obligatory classification, labelling and other information for a few thousand commonly-supplied chemical substances.
- The substances are listed in alphabetical order by name in Part I of the ASL (only these names may be used on the label, etc).
- The information given includes the classification, the label and, in some cases, specific concentration limit information.
- Full texts of the R- and S-phrases are given in Part V of the ASL together with other important information.

CLASSIFYING SUBSTANCES WHICH ARE NOT IN THE APPROVED SUPPLY LIST

37   This part of the guide may not be able to answer all of your questions. It will, however, explain where more detailed information can be found or help you identify the point at which you will need specialist help.

What you have to do

38   If you have been reading this guide from the beginning you will know that CHIP obliges suppliers to classify dangerous chemicals before they supply them. You will also know that the ASL contains EC-agreed classifications for a large number of commonly-supplied substances. But what do you do if the chemical you wish to supply is not in the ASL? The answer is that you must come up with a classification for it yourself. This is known as **self-classification.**

39   In this part of the guide we shall look at self-classification of substances and in the following part consider how to classify preparations. But first we must take some time to say what we mean by the words 'substance' and 'preparation'.

Substances and preparations

40   CHIP divides chemicals into two types: substances and preparations. These are mutually exclusive, so every chemical will be one or the other.

What is a substance?

41   Put simply a substance is a **single chemical** (for example, an element such as chlorine or a compound such as sodium hypochlorite). For exceptions to this definition see paragraph 43 below.

What is a preparation?

42   A preparation is a **mixture of substances** (for example, a paint). By a 'mixture' we mean the result of intentionally combining two or more substances, which do not react with each other to any appreciable extent, but simply co-exist. Usually such a mixture will combine the properties (both desirable and undesirable) of the constituents, although each is diluted by virtue of the others.

Mixtures which count as substances

43 Most mixtures are preparations but CHIP considers the following mixtures to be substances:

- those which consist of a main substance, together with an additive necessary to preserve stability or any impurity deriving from the production process (but not any solvent which may be removed without affecting the stability or composition of the main substance);
- many naturally occurring mixtures of chemicals, for example, plant-derived oils and petroleum or coal-derived chemicals which, in reality, are highly complex mixtures;
- chemicals in the ASL described as a 'mixture of substance A and substance B' or some defined solutions eg sulphuric acid. (All chemicals in the ASL are considered to be substances.)

Types of substance - existing and new

44 There are two types of substance you may have to classify:

- those listed on the *European Inventory of Existing Commercial Chemical Substances* (EINECS)[16] - known as **existing substances**; and
- all others - known as **new substances**.

EINECS is a list of about 100 000 substances which were on the European market in the 1980s. Because EINECS is a closed list, the status (existing or new) of a substance can never change. The European Chemicals Bureau maintains a searchable online version of EINECS. [16] Alternatively, you can contact HSE's Industrial Chemicals Unit (Tel: 0151 951 4000) for information on the status of particular substances.

Classification of new substances

45 A new substance (with certain exceptions described in the Regulations) must be notified to the national competent authority in accordance with the requirements of the Notification of New Substances Regulations 1993[17] (known as NONS) before it, or mixtures containing it, may be placed on the market. In the course of notification a classification and label is developed and must be used by the supplier. Notified new substances are listed on the *European List of Notified Chemical Substances* (ELINCS).[16] Eventually, they find their way on to the ASL and when this happens suppliers must use the classification and label given there.

46 Our experience is that if you are in the business of supplying new substances you use specialist expertise. If you have any problems, refer to the HSE publication *Making sense of NONS*.[18]

Classification of existing substances

Collecting relevant and accessible data

47 Before you may supply an existing substance which is not listed in the ASL you must, in accordance with regulation 4(4) and 4(5) of CHIP, search for relevant and accessible data on the substance and then classify it on the basis of that data using the criteria set out in the Approved Classification and Labelling Guide (ACLG).

48 The ACLG indicates that data for classification may come from:

● the results of previous tests (carried out by you or by others);

● information required by international rules on the transport of dangerous goods (for example, the substance may be listed in the Approved Carriage List (ACL)[19] issued in connection with the Carriage of Dangerous Goods (Classification, Packaging and Labelling) and Use of Transportable Pressure Receptacles Regulations 1996.[20] Many of the properties have similar criteria and inclusion in the ACL would suggest the substance was probably also dangerous for supply);

● reference works (this would include technical reference sources, such as textbooks, scientific/technical papers, trade journals, etc); and

● practical experience (for example, if you have had experience of the hazards posed by the substance being classified).

In addition, the results of validated structure-activity relationships (that is, scientifically inferring the dangers of a substance by comparing it with structurally similar substances whose dangers are known) and expert judgement may also be taken into account where appropriate.

Other sources which may be useful include HSE guidance such as Guidance Note EH40 - *Occupational exposure limits*,[21] the Risk Assessment document series EH72.[22] Professional institutions, trade associations, trades unions and specialist consultancies may all be sources of data.

49 The requirement in regulation 4(5) is to search for data - **there is no requirement to generate data by doing tests**. Thus, if, after making a full search, you find that you have no information on a particular dangerous effect you do not have to get a test done to see if the substance has that effect.

50 The next step is to compare the data with the hazard classification criteria in the ACLG. The classification criteria fall into three groups:

- physicochemical properties;
- health effects; and
- environmental effects.

Because a substance can meet more than one of the criteria it is important to consider all of them. If the data on the substance satisfy any of the criteria the substance is placed into the corresponding category of danger and the appropriate R-phrase is assigned. The criteria in the ACLG apply directly to data obtained by means of the test methods described in Annex V to the Dangerous Substances Directive[6] or by equivalent methods. In other cases, expert judgement should be used to evaluate data.

51 We shall not say much on this because the ACLG itself contains all the relevant information. However, to illustrate the principle let's say that in the course of your search for data on a substance you find the result of an acute toxicity test:

LD_{50} oral, rat 75 mg/kg

The paragraph headed 'Toxic' in the ACLG's section on health effects indicates that a substance with a rat oral LD_{50} value between 25 and 200 mg/kg should be placed into the category of danger 'Toxic' and assigned the risk phrase 'Toxic if swallowed'. Expressed in words, the classification is:

Toxic: Toxic if swallowed

in short it is:

T: R25

52   After working through the three groups of dangerous effects, and only if the substance has been classified into at least one category of danger (it doesn't matter which), you should consider whether to assign any of the ACLG's additional risk phrases. These phrases and their criteria are found in the sections of the ACLG entitled 'Other physicochemical properties' and 'Other health effects'.

53   See the flow chart below for a summary of the information in the previous paragraphs.

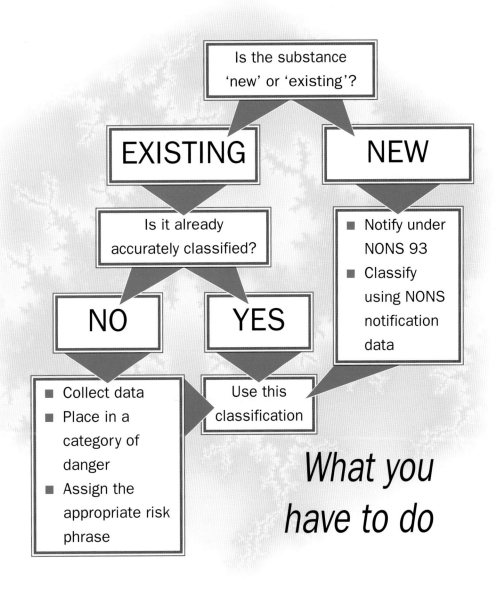

Is the substance 'new' or 'existing'?

EXISTING   NEW

Is it already accurately classified?

■ Notify under NONS 93
■ Classify using NONS notification data

NO   YES

■ Collect data
■ Place in a category of danger
■ Assign the appropriate risk phrase

Use this classification

What you have to do

Retention of data

54 CHIP no longer requires that a record of the information used for self-classification of a substance be kept for at least three years after it was last supplied. However, an HSE inspector (or a Trading Standards Officer if you sell direct to the public) may want to know how you have classified your substance and it would be useful to have this information to hand.

Summary of key points

- Substances are single chemicals. Preparations are mixtures of substances.
- Existing substances are those listed in EINECS.[16] New substances are all other substances.
- Supplier proposes a classification and label for a new substance during notification under NONS Regulations.[17]
- Supplier classifies an existing substance by:
  - collecting data (no need to carry out any tests); and
  - comparing data with classification criteria in ACLG to place substance into any relevant categories of danger and assign appropriate R-phrases.

CLASSIFYING PREPARATIONS

55   This part of the guide explains how to classify preparations. For the meaning of 'preparation' see paragraphs 40 to 43 in Part three. In what follows we shall use the terms 'constituent' and 'ingredient' interchangeably to mean any component of a preparation. Such components may be substances or preparations.

56   Preparations are the most common kind of chemical product. There is no limit to their number as, quite apart from the formulation of entirely new products, it is always possible to add another constituent to an existing product or to vary the proportions of the constituents. CHIP obliges anyone who supplies a dangerous preparation to classify it before it is supplied.

Overview

57   There are no preparations in the ASL so you must classify them yourself unless someone higher up the supply chain has done it for you. Remember, however, that you need to do quality checks before relying on another's classifications.

Methods of classification

58   You must classify a preparation for its dangerous physicochemical properties and its health and environmental effects. In general, there are two ways of doing this:

●   using an arithmetical procedure known as the **conventional method**, described in Schedule 3 to the Regulations; or

●   using the **classification criteria** in the *Approved Classification and Labelling Guide* (ACLG).

59   The first method resembles self-classification of substances (see Part three of this guide) in that you need data on the preparation's dangerous properties, eg its flash point temperature, LD_{50} values, etc. Usually there are no available data on a preparation so laboratory tests would be necessary if you intend to use this approach.

60   The second method is based on the idea that a preparation can be expected to have the same dangerous effect as a constituent if it contains enough of the constituent. To use this method you will need to know the classification of each constituent and use other information described later.

61   If you use both methods and the results differ you should use the result based on test data except for carcinogenic, mutagenic and toxic to reproduction effects where classification must always be by the conventional method.

62   We'll look first at classification on the basis of physicochemical properties and then health and environmental effects together. The detailed rules are in the ACLG (and Schedule 3 to the Regulations) so it will be helpful to have those documents to hand.

Classification on the basis of physicochemical properties

63   The aim is to decide whether the preparation should be placed into any of the categories of danger: explosive, oxidising, extremely flammable, highly flammable or flammable, and assigned the relevant symbol and R-phrases. The conventional method does not apply so, unless you assign the classification on the basis of adequate available data, you must get tests done (see paragraphs 67 and 68 for exceptions to testing).

64   The preparation should be:

● tested in accordance with the methods described in Annex V to the Dangerous Substances Directive;[6] and

● the test results compared to the classification criteria set out in the part of the ACLG entitled 'Classification on the basis of physicochemical properties'.

65   If you are unable to perform the tests yourself you should employ someone with the necessary facilities and expertise, eg a contract testing house. There are a number of methods for determining flash point and these can give widely differing results. Advice on the appropriate method to use can be sought on a case-by-case basis from HSE's Industrial Chemicals Unit (Tel: 0151 951 4000).

66   Once you have the test results you should compare them with the criteria in the ACLG to determine the classification. The ACLG contains all of the information needed to do this.

67   You need not test for a dangerous physicochemical property if:

● the preparation has no ingredients with that property; and

● you judge, on the basis of the information available to you, that the preparation is unlikely to have that property.

In such cases the preparation is not placed into the relevant category of danger or assigned the corresponding R-phrase. However, keep in mind that some preparations have dangerous physicochemical properties not possessed by any of their constituents. For example, gunpowder (a mixture of carbon, sulphur and potassium nitrate) is explosive even though none of its ingredients are.

A preparation consists of 80% water and 20% of acetone. Acetone is classified in the ASL as F: R11 ('Highly flammable') (and with various health effects not relevant to this example). The preparation could be flammable and should be tested for that property. However, it would not be necessary to test for explosivity or oxidation since acetone does not have these properties and there is no reason to suspect that a mixture of acetone and water would have them.

Calculation-based approaches

68   The conventional method is not applicable to physicochemical properties but some calculational approaches are available and described in the ACLG under 'Special cases'. They include an optional method for flammability of gases and two obligatory methods for the oxidising potential of gases and of organic peroxides.

Classification on the basis of health effects and environmental effects

69   The aim is to decide whether the preparation should be placed into any of the categories of danger: very toxic, toxic, harmful, corrosive, irritant, sensitising, carcinogenic, mutagenic, toxic for reproduction or dangerous for the environment and assigned the relevant R-phrases.

70   If a preparation has no constituents with dangerous health or environmental effects then it will not have these effects either. However, if it does have such constituents then you must assess whether the preparation is dangerous for health or the environment.

71   There are two ways of obtaining the classification: (1) by the use of the conventional method, or (2) by the use of test data and the criteria in the ACLG. The following restrictions apply:

●   **carcinogenic, mutagenic and toxic to reproduction effects** - you may only use the conventional method to classify for these effects;

●   **aspiration hazard (R65)** - you may only classify for this on the basis of test data (see the relevant part of the paragraph headed 'Harmful' in the ACLG);

●   **all other health effects** - you are free to use either the conventional method or test data and the criteria in the ACLG;

●   **environmental effects** - you must use the conventional method (but see paragraph 88 for an exception).

Classification on the basis of test data

72 The preparation should be:

- tested in accordance with the methods described in Annex V to the Dangerous Substances Directive;[6] and
- the test results compared to the classification criteria in the parts of the ACLG entitled 'Classification on the basis of health effects and Classification on the basis of environmental effects'.

73 If you are unable to perform the tests yourself you should employ someone with the necessary facilities and expertise, eg a contract testing house. Once you have the test results you should compare them with the criteria in the ACLG to determine the classification. The ACLG contains all of the information needed to do this.

Classification on the basis of the conventional method

74 The conventional method is applicable to both health and environmental effects. In order to use it you have to know:

- the **classification** of each dangerous constituent;
- the **concentration** of each dangerous constituent; and
- the **concentration** limits for the dangerous effects of each dangerous constituent.

Some key questions

Where do I get the classifications of the dangerous constituents?

75 Substances listed in the ASL have their classifications given there. Other substances should be self-classified as described in Part three of this guide. Where you have received a substance or a preparation from another supplier you may use their classification provided you make reasonable checks of its reliability.

What is the concentration of a dangerous constituent?

76 This is the proportion of the preparation that the constituent makes up. Concentrations should be calculated on a weight for weight basis for solid or liquid preparations, and on a volume for volume basis for gaseous preparations and expressed as percentages.

1 kg of a preparation contains 0.5 kg of water and 0.5 kg of substance X. The concentration of substance X is (0.5 kg)/(1.0 kg) = 50%.

What is a concentration limit?

77   This is the lowest concentration of a chemical with a given dangerous effect which causes a preparation containing that chemical to be deemed to have the effect. For example, the concentration limit for the effect represented by the phrase R52 ('Harmful to aquatic organisms') is 25%, so a preparation containing 25% or more of a substance assigned R52 would also be assigned R52.

78   Some dangerous effects give rise to a hierarchy of concentration limits corresponding to varying degrees of danger. For example, if a substance is classified as T+: R28 (very toxic by swallowing) then a preparation containing it will be classified as:

T+: R28, if the substance's concentration is greater than or equal to 7%;

T: R25 (toxic by swallowing), if greater than or equal to 1%; and

Xn: R22 (harmful by swallowing), if greater than or equal to 0.1%.

Types of concentration limit

79   There are two types of concentration limit:

- **specific concentration limits** which are assigned to some substances in the ASL and apply only to them; and
- **general concentration limits** which apply to the hazardous effects of any substance which has not been assigned specific concentration limits.

The general concentration limits are in Part II (health) and Part III (environmental) of Schedule 3 to the Regulations.

80   The procedure is set out in Part I of Schedule 3, from paragraph 5 onwards. Each paragraph deals with a different category of danger and gives the conditions for a preparation to be placed into that category. The basic idea is that you should read each paragraph in turn and check to see if your preparation meets the conditions for classification in that category. It will usually be obvious that some paragraphs can be omitted because they are not relevant to your preparation.

Using the conventional method

EXAMPLE 3

A preparation has an ingredient classified as very toxic and as a category 2 carcinogen. Which paragraphs in Part I are relevant in classifying the preparation?

Depending on its concentration, a very toxic ingredient may cause a preparation to be classified as very toxic, toxic or harmful. Consequently, paragraph 6 (classification as very toxic) should be checked first. If the condition there is not met, paragraph 7 (toxic) should be checked next and then paragraph 8 (harmful). If it meets none of these, the preparation is not classified for these effects.

An ingredient classified as a category 2 carcinogen may cause a preparation to be classified as a category 2 carcinogen but not as anything else. Therefore it is only necessary to check paragraph 13(1) (category 1 and 2 carcinogenic). It is not necessary to check 15(2) (category 3 carcinogenic) or any other paragraphs.

81   The conditions to be met for a preparation to be classified with a particular dangerous effect are of two types:

- classify the preparation if it contains an ingredient whose concentration is greater than or equal to the relevant concentration limit;
- classify the preparation if it contains a number of ingredients whose combined effect meet a condition expressed by a formula.

The first type applies to every dangerous effect. The second type applies only to some dangerous effects (known as additive effects).

82   As an example of how this works, look at paragraph 7 in Part I of Schedule 3 which gives conditions for classification of a preparation as 'very toxic'. This category of danger covers two types of dangerous effect:

- acute lethal effects; and
- non-lethal irreversible effects after a single exposure.

Acute lethal effects are those with the R-phrases identified in Table I/IA in Part II (ie R26, 27, 28 and their combinations). Non-lethal irreversible effects are those with R-phrases in Table II/IIA (ie R39/route(s) of exposure, eg R39/26).

Acute lethal effects are covered by sub-paragraph (1)(a) of paragraph 7 (a condition of the first type in paragraph 81) and sub-paragraph (b) (a condition of the second type in paragraph 81). Sub-paragraph (a) should be applied first. If this does not lead to classification, and if there is more than one very toxic ingredient, sub-paragraph (1)(b) should be tried. If this does not lead to classification then the preparation is not classified as very toxic for acute lethal effects. However, it may be toxic or harmful for these effects and the relevant sub-paragraphs in paragraphs 8 and 9 should be checked.

Non-lethal irreversible effects are covered by sub-paragraph (2) of paragraph 7 (a condition of the first type in paragraph 81). If this is not met then the preparation is not classified as very toxic for non-lethal irreversible effects. However, it may be toxic or harmful for these effects and the relevant sub-paragraphs in paragraphs 8 and 9 should be tried.

Additive effects

83   Notice that there is a formula (in sub-paragraph (1)(b)) for evaluating the combined effect of a number of ingredients with acute lethal effects but none for non-lethal irreversible effects. Effects like acute lethality which may be added up over all the ingredients sharing them are additive. The table below identifies additive and non-additive effects with their corresponding R-phrases.

Table of additive and non-additive dangerous effects	
Type of dangerous effect	*R-phrases for classification*
additive health effects	
acute lethal effects	**R20, R21, R22, R23, R24, R25, R26, R27, R28,** and combinations, eg **R20/21**
corrosive and irritant effects	**R34, R35, R36, R37, R38, R41,** and combinations, eg **R36/37**
additive environmental effects	
acute aquatic effects	**R50** and **R52**
long-term aquatic effects	**R53**
acute and long-term aquatic effects	**R50/53; R52/53**
non-additive health effects	
non-lethal irreversible effects after a single exposure	**R39**/route(s) of exposure (eg **R39/24**) and **R68**/route(s) of exposure (eg **R68/20**)
severe effects after repeated or prolonged exposure	**R48**/route(s) of exposure (eg **R48/20**)
sensitising effects	**R42, R43** and **R42/43**
carcinogenic, mutagenic and toxic to reproduction effects	**R40, R68, R45, R46, R49, R60, R61, R62,** and **R63**
non-additive environmental effects	
ozone depleting effects	**R59**

84 When using the conventional method it is important to work in an orderly way. In particular, it is a good idea to start by writing down all the ingredients of the preparation together with their concentrations, classifications and relevant concentration limits. A possible format is:

P r e p a r a t i o n A			
Name	**Conc**	**Classification**	**Conc limits**
Ingredient J	**15%**	**Xn: R22** **Xi: R36**	**≥25% then Xn: R22** **≥20% then Xi: R36**
Ingredient K	**20%**	**R42** **N: R50, 53**	**≥1% then R42** **≥25% then N: R50, 53** **<25% and ≥ 2.5% then N: R51, 53** **<2.5% and ≥ 0.2.5% then R52, 53**
Non-classified ingredient(s)	**65%**	**n/a**	**n/a**

(The symbols '≥' and '<' mean 'greater than or equal to' and 'less than' respectively.)

85 We'll now illustrate the conventional method with some examples. We'll deal with both health and environmental effects as there is no essential difference between these as far as the conventional method is concerned.

E X A M P L E   4

A preparation with one dangerous ingredient

P r e p a r a t i o n A			
Name	**Conc**	**Classification**	**Conc limits**
Substance X	**50%**	**Xn: R22**	**≥25% then Xn: R22**
Water	**50%**	**n/a**	**n/a**

Substance X is not in the ASL so we have used the general concentration limit for R22 which is 25% (see Table I in Part II of Schedule 3).

X is classified as harmful so it may mean the preparation is classified as harmful. To see if it does we refer to paragraph 9 (harmful) in Part I of Schedule 3. R22 is an acute lethal effect so sub-paragraphs (1)(a) and (b) are the relevant parts of paragraph 9. Sub-paragraph (1)(a) indicates that a preparation is harmful if it contains a harmful ingredient at a concentration greater than or equal to its harmful limit. X's concentration (=50%) is greater than its concentration limit for harmful (=25%) so we classify preparation A as harmful and assign R22 (ie as Xn: R22).

Note that if the concentration of substance X was reduced to less than the concentration limit the preparation would escape classification.

E X A M P L E   5

A liquid preparation with one dangerous ingredient and more than one concentration limit

Preparation B

Name	Conc	Classification	Conc limits
Substance Y	5%	T+: R28	≥7% then T+: R28 ≤7% and ≥1% then T: R25 <1% and ≥0.1% then Xn: R22
Non-classified ingredient(s)	95%	n/a	n/a

Substance Y is not in the ASL so we have used the general concentration limits for R28 as given in Table I in Part II of Schedule 3.

Y is very toxic and may cause the preparation to be very toxic, toxic or harmful. First we must check the possibility of very toxic so we look at paragraph 7. The relevant sub-paragraphs are (1)(a) and (b), as R28 is an acute lethal effect. The condition in (1)(a) is not met because the concentration of Y (=5%) is less than its very toxic limit (=7%). (1)(b) only applies if there is more than one very toxic ingredient which is not the case here. Therefore the preparation is not very toxic. We move on to consider paragraph 8 (toxic). The condition in 8(1)(a) is met as Y's concentration (=5%) is greater than its toxic limit (=1%) so we classify preparation B as toxic and assign R25 (ie T: R25).

Where an ingredient has multiple concentration limits it can be helpful to refer to these limits by name. For substance Y, 7%, 1% and 0.1% are respectively its very toxic, toxic and harmful limits.

E X A M P L E   6

A preparation with another preparation as an ingredient

Preparation C (description 1)

Name	Conc	Classification	Conc limits
Preparation A	40%	Xn: R22	≥25% then Xn: R22
Water	60%	n/a	n/a

Preparation C (description 2)

Name	Conc	Classification	Conc limits
Substance X	20%	Xn: R22	≥25% then X n: R22
Water	80%	n/a	n/a

The procedure to classify C is the same as described in Example 4. However, the result is different depending on which description of C we use. Description 1 leads to classification as Xn: R22 and description 2 leads to non-classification.

Neither of these classifications is wrong and either can be used. The difference between them is due to the fact that description 1 did not take account of the large amount of water in preparation A. If you wish to avoid possible overclassification of a preparation which contains other preparations you should use the most detailed breakdown of it you can. This may involve working closely with your suppliers.

A preparation with two ingredients with a non-additive effect

Preparation D

Name	Conc	Classification	Conc limits
Substance P	0.75%	R43	≥1% then R43
Substance Q	0.75%	R43	≥1% then R43
Non-classified ingredient(s)	98.5%	n/a	n/a

Sensitisation - both skin sensitisation and respiratory sensitisation - is covered by paragraph 12 in Part 1 of Schedule 3.

Paragraph 12 says that a preparation should be classified with R43 if it has an ingredient classified with R43 whose concentration is greater than or equal to its concentration limit for R43. Because the concentrations of P and Q (=0.75%) are each less than their concentration limit (=1%) preparation D is not classified.

Notice that the preparation is not classified even though it contains 1.5% of skin sensitisers. Skin sensitisation is not an additive effect so classification is always considered one ingredient at a time.

A preparation with two ingredients with an additive effect

Preparation E

Name	Conc	Classification	Conc limits
Substance R	15%	Xi: R38	≥20% then Xi: R38
Substance S	15%	Xi: R38	≥25% then Xi: R38
Water	70%	n/a	n/a

Substance R is in the ASL without specific concentration limits so we use the general concentration limit for R38 from Table IV in Part II of Schedule 3. S is in the ASL with a specific concentration limit for R38.

R38 ('Irritating to the skin') is covered by paragraph 11 in Part I. The relevant sub-paragraphs are (3)(a) and (b). Paragraph 11(3)(a) indicates that a preparation is classified as Xi: R38 if it contains corrosive (R34 or R35) ingredients or skin-irritating ingredients (R38) which are present at or above their irritant limit. It is clear that E has no corrosive ingredients and although R and S are skin irritants their concentrations (=15%) are less than their irritant limits (=20% and 25% respectively). Thus neither R nor S on its own classifies the preparation, but irritancy is an additive effect so we can and should consider their combined effect.

Turning to sub-paragraph (b) we see that a preparation should be classified as a skin irritant, ie as Xi: R38, if the following condition is met:

$$\Sigma \left(\frac{P_{C:R35}}{L_{Xi:R38}} + \frac{P_{C:R34}}{L_{Xi:R38}} + \frac{P_{Xi:R38}}{L_{Xi:R38}} \right) \geq 1$$

where:

$P_{C:R35}$ is the concentration of each corrosive ingredient with R35 ('Causes severe burns')

$P_{C:R34}$ is the concentration of each corrosive ingredient with R34 ('Causes burns')

$P_{Xi:R38}$ is the concentration of each irritant ingredient with R38

$L_{Xi:R38}$ is the irritant (R38) concentration limit for each ingredient

The formula appears complex but in fact it contains only some divisions, additions and a simple comparison. To apply it we must:

(1a)   work out the fraction $P_{C:R35}/L_{Xi:R38}$ for each corrosive ingredient with R35

(1b)   work out the fraction $P_{C:R34}/L_{Xi:R38}$ for each corrosive ingredient with R34

(1c)   work out the fraction $P_{Xi:R38}/L_{Xi:R38}$ for each irritant ingredient with R38

(2)   add up all of these fractions

(3)   if the total is greater than or equal to 1 classify the preparation as Xi: R38

Following the steps we have:

(1a)   there are no corrosive ingredients with R35 so we ignore the first term in the formula

(1b)   there are no corrosive ingredients with R34 so we ignore the second term in the formula

(1c)   for substance R: $P_{Xi:R38}$ = 15% and $L_{Xi:R38}$ = 20% so $P_{Xi:R38}/L_{Xi:R38}$ = 15%/20% = 0.75

for substance S: $P_{Xi:R38}$ = 15% and $L_{Xi:R38}$ = 25% so $P_{Xi:R38}/L_{Xi:R38}$ = 15%/25% = 0.6

(2)   0.75 + 0.6 = 1.35

(3)   because 1.35 is greater than 1 preparation E is classified as Xi: R38

Notice that if the concentration of S is reduced to 5% then $P_{Xi:R38}/L_{Xi:R38}$ = 5%/25% = 0.2 and because 0.75 + 0.2 = 0.95 is less than 1 the preparation would escape classification.

Lower limits of concentration

86   Lower limits of concentration are cut-off concentrations below which ingredients do not have to be taken into account when working out the classification of a preparation. For example, if a preparation has a number of irritant ingredients only those whose individual concentrations are 1% or more will be considered when classifying the preparation for irritancy. There is a table of lower limits of concentration in paragraph 6 of Part I of Schedule 3 to the Regulations.

E X A M P L E   9

A preparation with an ingredient whose concentration is less than the lower limit of concentration

P r e p a r a t i o n   F

Name	Conc	Classification	Conc limits
Substance U	4.5%	C: R35	≥10% then C: R35 <10% and ≥ 5% then C: R34 <5% and ≥ 1% then Xi: R36/38
Substance V	0.5%	C: R35	≥10% then C: R35 <10% and ≥ 5% then C: R34 <5% and ≥ 1% then Xi: R36/38
Water	95%	n/a	n/a

U and V are in the ASL without specific concentration limits so we use the general concentration limits given in Table IV and VI in Part II of Schedule 3.

The lower limit of concentration for substances classified as corrosive (R34 or R35) is 1%. Therefore we do not take any account of substance V when classifying F for corrosive or irritant effects. Consequently, F is classified as Xi: R36/38 by virtue of the presence of U.

Assigning appropriate R-phrases

87   The formulas at paragraphs 7(1)(b), 8(1)(b) and 9(1)(b) in Part II of Schedule 3 determine whether a preparation containing a number of ingredients with acute lethal effects should be classified as very toxic, toxic or harmful. However, unlike the other formulas, they leave the choice of R-phrase(s) up to you. The following example illustrates the approach to be taken in such cases.

E X A M P L E   1 0

Preparation G

Name	Conc	Classification	Conc limits
Substance G1	0.5%	T+: R28	≥7% then T+: R28 <7% and ≥ 1% then T: R25 <1% and ≥ 0.1% then Xn: R22
Substance G2	15%	T: R24	≥25% then T: R24 <25% and ≥ 3% then Xn: R21
Water	84.5%	n/a	n/a

It is clear that G1 on its own does not classify the preparation as very toxic or toxic because in both cases its concentration is less than its concentration limits. G2 also does not classify the preparation as toxic for the same reason. However, before we can leave toxic and consider harmful we must consider the combined effect of G1 and G2 (R28 and R24 are acute lethal effects and therefore additive). Paragraph 8(1)(b) in Part II of Schedule 3, indicates that a preparation should be classified as toxic if:

$$\Sigma \left(\frac{P_{T+}}{L_T} + \frac{P_T}{L_T} \right) \geq 1$$

Where:

P_{T+} is the concentration of each very toxic ingredient with acute lethal effects

P_T is the concentration of each toxic ingredient with acute lethal effects

L_T is the toxic limit for each ingredient with acute lethal effects

Applying the formula we have:

(1)   for substance G1: P_{T+} = 0.5% and L_T = 1% so P_{T+}/L_T = 0.5%/1% = 0.5

         for substance G2: P_T = 15% and LT = 25% so P_T/L_T = 15%/25% = 0.6

(2)   0.5 + 0.6 = 1.1

(3)   because 1.1 is greater than 1 preparation G is classified as toxic (ie T)

What R-phrase(s) should be assigned? G1 is very toxic if swallowed (R28) and G2 is toxic in contact with skin (R24). The preparation G is toxic by virtue of the presence of G1 and G2 and its classification should reflect their routes of exposure, ie oral and through skin. We need R-phrases which describe toxic effects by these routes. The relevant R-phrases are R24 and R25 (R25 is Toxic by swallowing) and we classify the preparation as T: R24/25.

Note that T: R24/28 would be incorrect as R28 means very toxic by swallowing which cannot legitimately be combined with T.

This concludes the examples illustrating the conventional method.

Exception to the use of the conventional method when classifying for environmental effects

88   We mentioned in paragraph 71 that there was an exception to the requirement that you must always use the conventional method to classify for environmental effects. This exception allows you to test your preparation and then use the criteria in the ACLG to classify it. It applies only to assessment of acute aquatic toxicity and is subject to the following condition (except in the case of preparations subject to the Plant Protection Products Regulations, [23] where other requirements may apply):

● the preparation must be tested on all three test species (algae, daphnia and fish) unless testing on one species determines classification at the highest hazard classification.

Retention of data

89   Regulation 12 of CHIP requires that a record of the information used for the classification of a preparation be kept for at least three years. A copy of the information must be made available to an HSE inspector if requested (or to a Trading Standards Officer if you sell direct to the public). There is no standard format for this data and it may be kept electronically if desired.

Summary of key points

● Classify for physicochemical properties on the basis of test data.
● Classify for health and environmental effects on the basis of either test data or the conventional method, but subject to the restrictions set out in paragraph 71.
● Keep record of information used to classify for at least three years.

SUPPLY LABELLING

Legal requirements

90   We hope that most people will be able to draw up labels using just the advice in this guide. If you need to refer to the relevant section of CHIP then regulations 9 and 10 and Schedule 5 are the main parts on labelling. The ACLG also contains information on labelling.

What do you have to label?

91   Only packages (and any outer layer of packaging, other than that used solely for transport purposes) have to be labelled with CHIP labels. If you supply a chemical in bulk or down a pipeline then it does not need to be labelled (although you will still have to provide a safety data sheet).

Combined supply and carriage labelling

92   This guide does not cover carriage labelling. This is now dealt with by the Carriage of Dangerous Goods (Classification, Packaging and Labelling) and Use of Transportable Pressure Receptacles Regulations 1996.[20] Rules for combined supply and carriage labels are in regulations 9 and 10 of those Regulations.

How do you label it?

93   It is important that the label is clear and has impact. The label should be:

● securely fixed to the package with its entire surface in contact with the package, or directly printed onto the package;

● clearly and indelibly printed;

● designed so that the information on it can be easily read; and

● designed so that the symbol or symbols stand out and are easily noticed.

What size should the label be?

94   The size of the label depends on the size of the package. The requirements are:

Capacity of package	Label size
3 l or less	if possible at least 52 x 74 mm
3 l but <2 l	at least 74 x 105 mm
50 l but < 500 l	at least 105 x 148 mm
500 l	at least 148 x 210 mm

You are not obliged to set this information out on a separate label or in a separate part of your product label, but the table shows the minimum area that you must devote to this information.

95   On this matter the text of CHIP closely follows that of an EC Directive, which unfortunately is capable of being interpreted in more than one way. Some people consider that each symbol should be at least 10% of the *minimum* size of the label as specified above, the symbols could therefore be less than 10% of the *actual* size of the label if the label was larger than the minimum. However, we think that each symbol should be at least 10% of the actual size of the label. Some EC countries have drafted their law to make this an explicit requirement. Because it is a grey area in CHIP, suppliers may make their own choice.

96   The only part of the label which has a colour specification is the symbol. This should be black on an orange/yellow background. The precise shade is left for you to choose.

97   This depends whether you are labelling a substance or a preparation:

The following information should be included on a label for a substance (the layout is not obligatory):

Glutaraldehyde		
 **Toxic**	 **Dangerous for the environment**	Toxic by inhalation and if swallowed Causes burns May cause sensitisation by inhalation and by skin contact Very toxic to aquatic organisms Keep locked up and out of the reach of children In case of contact with eyes, rinse immediately with plenty of water and seek medical advice Wear suitable protective clothing, gloves and eye/face protection
EC label 203-856-5		In case of accident or if you feel unwell seek medical advice immediately (show the label where possible) Avoid release to the environment. Refer to special instructions/safety data sheet
Supplied by: Dyson-Warner Chemicals Ltd, Dyne Close, Blainey, Ryanshire CH1P 3EX 0207 7170000		

- the name, address and telephone number of a supplier in the European Economic Area (EEA);*

- the name of the substance. If the name is in the ASL, one of the names listed there should be used. If not, an internationally recognised name should be used. This should be a chemical name and not a trade name;

- the indication(s) of danger and the corresponding symbol(s) (these can be found in

---

*The EEA consists of the European Union plus Norway, Iceland and Liechtenstein.

Schedule 2 to CHIP). If your substance is classified into two or more categories with different symbols then Part I of Schedule 5 to CHIP tells you which ones you need to put on the label;

- the risk phrases. These are part of the classification, which should have been determined before labelling. Each risk phrase should appear in full, there is no need for its number, eg R20, to appear as well. Advice on the selection of risk phrases can be found in the ACLG although there is no general rule on the number of risk phrases that should appear on the label. If the risk phrase is the same as one of the indications of danger (eg extremely flammable, highly flammable or flammable), it does not have to be repeated;

- the safety phrases. Advice on the selection of these can be found in the ACLG. Each safety phrase should appear in full, there is no need for its number. As a general rule, no more than six safety phrases should appear on the label;

- the EC number. For a substance listed in the ASL, this is the number given there. For an existing substance not listed in the ASL (or listed in the ASL without an EC number), use the EINECS number (found in the European Inventory of Existing Commercial Chemical Substances).[16] For a new substance not listed in the ASL (or listed in the ASL without an EC number), use the ELINCS number (found in the European List of Notified Chemical Substances).[16] If you don't have access to EINECS or ELINCS contact HSE's Industrial Chemicals Unit (Tel: 0151 951 4000);

- if the substance is in the ASL, the label should bear the words 'EC label'. This indicates the classification and label have been agreed by EC Member States.

Preparation   The following information should be included on a label for a preparation (the layout is not obligatory):

Cellulose Spraypaint
Full Gloss Golden Yellow
Contains, Toluene, C. I. Pigment Yellow 34
Contains lead. Should not be used on surfaces that are liable to be chewed or sucked by children.

Toxic   **Dangerous for the environment**   **Highly Flammable**

Harmful by Inhalation.
May cause harm to the unborn child.
Danger of cumulative effects.
Limited evidence of a carcinogenic effect.
Possible risk of impaired fertility.
Very toxic to aquatic organisms, may cause long-term adverse effects in the aquatic environment.

Keep container tightly closed.
Wear suitable protective clothing, gloves and eye/face protection.
If swallowed, seek medical advice immediately and show this container or label.
Avoid exposure - Obtain special instructions before use.

Avoid release to the environment. Refer to special instructions/safety data sheet. Do not breathe vapour or spray.
In case of insufficient ventilation wear suitable respiratory equipment.
Restricted to professional users.   1 litre

Supplied by:
Dyson-Warner Chemicals Ltd, Moore Close, Blainey, Ryanshire CH1P 3EX
0207 7170000

- The name, address and telephone number of a supplier in the EEA.

- The trade name or other designation of the preparation.

- The names of the main dangerous ingredients in the preparation according to the rules laid down in Part I of Schedule 5 to CHIP 3.

- The indication or indications of danger and the corresponding symbols (these can be found in Schedule 2 to CHIP 3).

- The risk phrases (as for substances). As a general rule, no more than six risk phrases should appear on the label.

- The safety phrases (as for substances).

- If the preparation is to be sold to the general public, the nominal quantity.

- There are also additional labelling requirements if the preparation contains specific substances (such as isocyanates) or is used in a specific way (eg by spraying). More details of these can be found in Part II of Schedule 5 to CHIP.

Are there any circumstances where I need to label if my preparation is not classified as dangerous?

98 In a few specific cases a label will be required on a preparation even if it isn't classified as dangerous. More details of these preparations can be found in Part I of Schedule 5 to CHIP.

Do I have to take any action if my preparation contains a sensitiser but is not classified as sensitising?

99 Yes, Part II of Schedule 5 to CHIP 3 requires suppliers to label the packaging of preparations containing at least one substance classified as sensitising (present in a concentration $\geq 0.1\%$ or in a concentration specified under a specific note in its ASL entry) with:

'Contains (name of sensitising substance(s)). May produce an allergic reaction.'

Are there any exceptions to the labelling requirements for substances and preparations?

100 There are some important exceptions to the requirement to label a dangerous chemical. Full details of these can be found in regulations 8 and 10 of CHIP 3. However, remember that these are exceptions to labelling only, the chemical will still be classified and you may have to provide a safety data sheet to professional users. Basically, the position is:

- If the classification of the chemical is explosive, very toxic, toxic, carcinogenic, mutagenic, toxic to reproduction, or sensitising then you always have to label the package in full.

- If the classification of the chemical is harmful, extremely flammable, highly flammable, flammable, irritant or oxidising then you do not have to label it for that hazardous property if the quantity is so small that there is no foreseeable risk, relating to that hazardous property, of danger to people. This includes both someone handling the substance and others who could be vulnerable people such as children.

- If the classification of your *preparation* is dangerous for the environment (with or without the N symbol) then you do not have to label it in respect of its environmental hazard if the quantity is so small that there is no foreseeable risk, under conditions of supply, use and disposal, of danger to the environment (regulation 8(10) of CHIP). (Note that this provision only applies to preparations, not to substances.)

- If the package contains less than 125 ml of the chemical which is a:
  - *substance* classified only as harmful (unless it is supplied to the general public), highly flammable, flammable, irritant or oxidising, the risk and safety phrases do not have to be shown (regulation 8(11) of CHIP).
  - *preparation* classified only as highly flammable, irritant (except those assigned the phrase R41), dangerous for the environment and assigned the N symbol, or oxidising, the risk and safety phrases do not have to be shown (regulation 8(12) of CHIP);
  - *preparation* classified only as flammable or as dangerous for the environment (and not assigned the N symbol), then only the R-phrases need to be shown, that is to say the safety phrases need not be shown (as there is no symbol/indication of danger the risk phrase is needed to tell you what the danger is).

- The label does not have to have its entire surface in contact with the package if the package is an awkward shape or too small. The label may be attached to the package in some other appropriate way (regulation 10(7) of CHIP). This could be by a fold out (concertina) label or a tag. The label should be securely attached and resistant to damage. It is essential that the part of the label which sets out the classification is visible to a prospective purchaser. You can put the safety phrases on a separate sheet which accompanies the package if the container is an awkward shape or so small that they cannot be put on the label.

Can I keep any constituents of my preparation confidential?

101 There are limited provisions for this in CHIP Schedule 5, Part 1, paragraph 3. Where the person responsible for placing a preparation on the market wishes to take advantage of this, that person has to make a formal request. In the case of the UK, you must apply to HSE to take advantage of confidentiality provisions, enclosing the information specified in Annex VI to Council Directive 1999/45/EC. Further information can be obtained from HSE's Industrial Chemicals Unit, Confidentiality Team, Room 211, Magdalen House, Stanley Precinct, Bootle, Merseyside L20 3QZ (Tel: 0151 951 3295; email ukconf@hse.gsi.gov.uk), quoting CHIP 3: confidential preparations).

Some general points

102 Descriptions such as 'non-toxic', 'non-flammable', 'non-harmful', non-polluting', 'ecological' or any statement that may mislead people about the danger of the chemicals are not allowed on the packages of dangerous (ie classified) substances or preparations.

103 The label should be in English. However, if you are supplying chemicals in more than one Member State of the EEA, you might wish to provide the labelling information in more than one language. If you do so, you need to pay attention to the requirements for clarity and impact of the label in regulation 9 of CHIP. The label should have corresponding blocks for each language. Make sure you meet the minimum requirements for size and clarity. In addition, you must bear in mind that all the EU Member States have their own legislation on this subject. It is all based on the same European law as CHIP, but there may be minor differences and you should ensure your label follows the rules of the Member State(s) where it is marketed.

PACKAGING AND ADVERTISING

104 Regulation 8 of CHIP requires that the package containing a dangerous chemical should:

- prevent escape of the chemical;
- not be adversely affected by the chemical; and
- be strong enough to withstand normal handling.

In addition, if the package has a replaceable closure this must continue to prevent escape even after repeated use. The requirements of regulation 8 are considered satisfied if the packaging meets the relevant standards required by legislation on the carriage of dangerous goods.

Special packaging requirements

Child-resistant fastenings (CRFs)

105 Regulation 12 of CHIP sets out a number of special requirements in respect of packaging.

106 Child-resistant fastenings are package closures designed to prevent children from gaining access to dangerous chemicals. Regulation 11 requires that any recloseable packaging in which a dangerous chemical is supplied (to the general public) must have a child-resistant fastening if the chemical is:

- a substance or preparation required to be labelled with the indications of danger: very toxic, toxic or corrosive;
- a preparation containing 3% or more (by weight) of methanol;

- a preparation containing 1% or more (by weight) of dichloromethane; or
- a preparation which has been assigned labelling phrase R65 ('Harmful: may cause lung damage if swallowed') (unless the preparation is supplied in an aerosol dispenser or a container fitted with a sealed spray attachment).

You do not need a child-resistant fastening if you can show that a child cannot gain access to the chemical without the help of a tool.

107 Additionally, the packaging for any chemical in any of the four classes identified above must not have a shape or designation likely to attract the active curiosity of children or mislead consumers. This applies regardless of whether the packaging is recloseable or not.

Tactile warning devices (TWDs)

108 Tactile warning devices (normally small raised triangles) are intended to warn the visually impaired that they are handling a dangerous chemical.

109 Regulation 11 requires that any packaging (recloseable or non-recloseable) in which a dangerous substance or preparation is supplied to the general public must have a tactile warning device if the substance or preparation is required to be labelled with any of the indications of danger: very toxic, toxic, corrosive, harmful, extremely flammable or highly flammable.

Standards

110 Both child-resistant fastenings and tactile warning devices must meet certain standards. This is BS EN ISO 11683[24] for TWDs. You could be asked by a Trading Standards Officer for proof that CRFs meet the standard. You can make sure that they do by having them tested by an approved testing house (one that conforms to BS EN ISO/IEC 17025:2000[25]), which will give you a test certificate confirming that the standard has been met.

111 If you are still unclear about what needs to be done, you should first contact your local Trading Standards Office for advice. For further information, see the leaflet *Stop children swallowing household chemicals.*[26]

Advertising

112 Regulation 6 of CHIP requires that where an advertisement enables a member of the general public to conclude a contract to buy a dangerous chemical before seeing the package label (eg mail order or via the internet), the advertisement must mention the category of danger, the R-phrases and any special labelling phrase required under Part II of Schedule 5 (eg 'Warning. Contains lead').

SAFETY DATA SHEETS

hat is a safety data sheet?

113 CHIP requires suppliers to provide recipients of classified substances or preparations (and in some cases, preparations which are not classified) with a document, known as a safety data sheet (SDS) with information organised under 16 standard headings. This gives the recipient the information necessary to take measures relating to health and safety at work and the protection of the environment. SDS are useful in many situations, but are particularly important to workplace users of chemicals who rely on them when meeting duties under the *Control of Substances Hazardous to Health Regulations 1999* (COSHH)[12] to assess and control the risks arising from the use of dangerous chemicals. For this reason they are sometimes called 'COSHH sheets'. Safety data sheets have to be provided no matter how the chemical is supplied - in bulk or in packages.

When must safety data sheets be supplied?

lassified substances and preparations

114 This varies between classified substances and preparations and non-classified preparations, as described below.

115 Classified substances and preparations are those which have been placed into at least one category of danger and assigned an R-phrase. A SDS must be supplied with any classified substance or preparation which is supplied for use at work (the recipient does not have to request it). It should be supplied no later than the first delivery of the chemical and be free of charge. The SDS may be supplied in electronic form only if the supplier has established that the recipient is able to receive and read it in that way.

116 It is not necessary to supply a SDS to a member of the general public who buys a classified substance or preparation through a shop and does not intend to use it in the course of work (eg for DIY). However, you must provide that person with sufficient information about protection of health and safety (ie from the CHIP label and any supplementary labelling and/or information sheet).

Preparations which are not classified

117 If you supply a preparation which, although not classified, contains not less than 1% by weight (or 0.2% by volume for gaseous preparations) of any:

- dangerous substance which has been classified with health or environmental effects; or
- substance which has a Community workplace exposure limit,

you must supply a professional user (ie someone who will use the preparation in the course of work) with a copy of a safety data sheet containing proportionate information on the preparation **if they request it**. Additionally, the package must bear the labelling phrase 'Safety data sheet available for professional user on request'.

118 You do not have to supply the SDS to a member of the general public who buys the preparation through a shop and does not intend to use it in the course of work (eg for DIY), as long as you provide that person with sufficient information about protection of health and safety (ie from the CHIP label and any supplementary information sheet).

What information should be on the safety data sheet?

119 Apart from the date of first publication and the 16 obligatory headings (which are listed in Schedule 4 to CHIP), CHIP does not specify what information should go on the SDS. Instead, it requires that the information provided is sufficient to enable the user of the chemical to protect health, safety and the environment. It is for you (the supplier) to judge what amount and type of information is sufficient and in doing so you should take into account whatever you may know of the ways your customers use the product. To guide you in complying with the law, the Health and Safety Commission has issued an Approved Code of Practice,[5] which sets out under each of the 16 headings the type of information that might be expected. You do not have to follow this advice and are free to give other information. However, if you are prosecuted for not meeting the requirement to provide sufficient information and have not followed the code then a court will find you at fault unless you can show that you have complied with the requirement in some other way.

120 The use of the expression 'proportionate information' in connection with the SDS for preparations which have not been classified, but which contain small amounts of dangerous chemicals, allows for the possibility that the SDS may be less detailed than for classified preparations. The level of detail should be judged against what is needed to enable the user to protect health, safety and the environment.

Keeping the safety data sheet up-to-date and informing your customers of changes

121 You must keep any SDS you produce up-to-date. This means that if you become aware of significant new information relevant to health, safety or the environment in relation to the chemical you must amend the SDS accordingly and mark it with the word 'Revision' and the date of revision. Then you must provide a free copy of the revised SDS to every person who received a copy of the previous version within the last year and ensure that their attention is drawn to whatever is different in the revised version. This applies equally to SDS for classified substances and preparations and preparations which are not classified.

122 You may be able to use the SDSs your suppliers give you to produce your own SDSs. You may be able simply to photocopy them and pass them on when you supply the chemicals. However, **as a supplier you are responsible for the accuracy of the SDS** and there are some checks you should make:

● check that all the necessary headings in Schedule 4 to CHIP are in the SDS (these are also listed in the ACOP);

● check that the SDS is comparable to those for similar products;

● check that the sections dealing with safe use/storage etc are adequate for the intended applications of your customers; and

● check that the SDS covers all foreseeable eventualities.

If you have any doubts, talk to your supplier and think about what information your customers will need. You may wish to talk to your customers as well.

REFERENCES

1   *Chemicals (Hazard Information and Packaging for Supply) Regulations* 2002
SI 2002/1689 The Stationery Office 2002 ISBN 0 11 042419 0

2   *CHIP 2 for everyone* HSG126 HSE Books 1995 ISBN 0 7176 0857 3

3   *Approved supply list. Information approved for the classification and labelling of
substances and preparations dangerous for supply. Chemicals (Hazard Information and
Packaging for Supply) Regulations 2002* Approved list L129 (Seventh edition)
HSE Books 2002 ISBN 0 7176 2368 8

4   *Approved classification and labelling guide. Guidance on Regulations* L131 (Fifth
edition) HSE Books 2002 ISBN 0 7176 2369 6

5   *The compilation of safety data sheets. Approved Code of Practice* L130 HSE Books
2002 ISBN 0 7176 2371 8

6   Council Directive 67/548/EEC of 27 June 1967 on the approximation of laws,
regulations and administrative provisions relating to the classification, packaging and
labelling of dangerous substances *Official Journal* P 196, 16 August 1967 p1-98

7   *Idiot's guide to CHIP* Leaflet INDG350 HSE Books 2002 (single copy free or priced
packs of 10 ISBN 0 7176 2333 5)

8   *Read the label* Leaflet INDG352 HSE Books 2002 (single copy free or priced packs of
10 ISBN 0 7176 2366 1)

9   *Why do I need a safety data sheet?* Leaflet INDG353 HSE Books 2002 (single copy
free or priced packs of 10 ISBN 0 7176 2367 X)

10   *Chemicals (Hazard Information and Packaging) Regulations 1993* SI 1993/1746 The
Stationery Office 1993 ISBN 0 11 034746 3

11   *Chemicals (Hazard Information and Packaging) Regulations 1994* SI 1994/3247 The
Stationery Office 1994 ISBN 0 11 043877 9

12 *Control of Substances Hazardous to Health Regulations 1999 SI 1999/437* The Stationery Office 1999 ISBN 0 11 082087 8

13 *Are you involved in the carriage of dangerous goods by road or rail?* Leaflet INDG234(rev) HSE Books 1999 (single copy free or priced packs of 10 ISBN 0 7176 1676 2)

14 *Carriage of dangerous goods explained: Part 1 Guidance for consignors of dangerous goods by road and rail. Classification, packaging, labelling and provision of information* HSG160 HSE Books 1996 ISBN 0 7176 1255 4

15 Council Regulation (EEC) No 2455/92 of 23 July 1992 concerning the export and import of certain dangerous chemicals *Official Journal* L 251, 29 August 1992 p 13 - 22

16 *European Inventory of Existing Commercial Chemical Substances* available on the European Chemicals Bureau website at ecb.ei.jrc.it/existing-chemicals
European List of Notified Chemical Substances available on the European Chemicals Bureau website at ecb.jrc.it/new-chemicals

17 *Notification of New Substances Regulations* 1993 SI 1993/3050 The Stationery Office 1993 ISBN 0 11 034278 X

18 *Making sense of NONS: A guide to the Notification of New Substances Regulations 1993* HSG117 HSE Books 1994 ISBN 0 7176 0774 7

19 *Approved carriage list. Information approved for the carriage of dangerous goods by road and rail other than explosives and radioactive material. Approved list* L90 (Third edition) HSE Books 1999 ISBN 0 7176 1681 9

20 *Carriage of Dangerous Goods (Classification, Packaging and Labelling) and Use of Transportable Pressure Receptacles Regulations 1996 SI 1996/2092* The Stationery Office 1996 ISBN 0 11 062923 X

21 *Occupational exposure limits* EH40/2002 HSE Books 2001 ISBN 0 7176 2083 2

22 *Phenylhydrazine: Risk assessment document* EH72/1 HSE Books 1997 ISBN 0 7176 1355 0
Dimethylaminoethanol (DMAE): Risk assessment document EH72/2 HSE Books 1997 ISBN 0 7176 1356 9

Bromoethane: Risk assessment document EH72/3 HSE Books 1997 ISBN 0 7176 1357 7

3-Chloropropene: Risk assessement document EH72/4 HSE Books 1997 ISBN 0 7176 1353 4

a-Chlorotoluene: Risk assessment document EH72/5 HSE Books 1997 ISBN 0 7176 1354 2

2-Furaldehyde: Risk assessment document EH72/6 HSE Books 1997 ISBN 0 7176 1358 5

1,2-Diaminoethane (Ethylenediamine EDA): Risk assessment document EH72/7
HSE Books 1997 ISBN 0 7176 1338 0

Aniline: Risk assessment document EH72/8 HSE Books 1998 ISBN 0 7176 1526 X

Barium sulphate: Risk assessment document EH72/9 HSE Books 1998 ISBN 0 7176 1527 8

N-Methyl-2-Pyrrolidone: Risk assessment document EH72/10 HSE Books 1998 ISBN 0 7176 1528 6

Flour dust: Risk assessment document EH72/11 HSE Books 1999 ISBN 0 7176 2479 X

Bromochloromethane EH72/12 HSE Books 2000 ISBN 0 7176 1842 0

Methyl cyanoacrylate and ethyl cyanoacrylate: Risk assessment document EH72/13
HSE Books 2000 ISBN 0 7176 1843 9

Chlorine dioxide: Risk assessment document EH72/14 HSE Books 2000 ISBN 0 7176 1844 7

23   Plant Protection Products Regulations 1995 SI 1995/887 The Stationery Office 1995
ISBN 0 11 052865 4

24   British Standards Institution BS EN ISO 11683:1997 *Packaging. Tactile warnings of danger. Requirements*

25   British Standards Institution BS EN ISO/IEC 17025:2000 *General requirements for the competence of testing and calibration laboratories*

26   *Stop children swallowing household chemicals* Department of Trade and Industry available from the Consumer Safety Unit (Tel: 020 7215 3340)

Scratch and sniff .... chemical risks at work Video HSE Books 2002 ISBN 0 7176 22525

Further information

Printed and published by the Health and Safety Executive   C100   8/02